CHA

G000075631

the WORLD *in*

or

$10 LESS

STEPHANIE CANSIAN

Stephanie Cansian / Say It Simply Productions

stephanie@sayitsimplyproductions.com

Change the World in $10 or Less / Stephanie Cansian — 1st ed.

ISBN 979-8-9853969-1-1

Dedication

To everyone who thinks they can't.

Yes, you can.

Dedication

Like everyone else, my life drastically changed in 2020. Overnight my husband and I became both essential workers and homeowners. We started taking things day by day, being thankful that we weren't sick and still had jobs, in that order. When groceries got scarce, we got creative. When we couldn't visit friends and family, we video called. For all of 2020, we made it work.

However, in January 2021, I finally broke down. I was mismanaged, disrespected, and generally unhappy at my office job. At the end of the day, I was so exhausted that I didn't have spoons left for anything else: not my writing, not my family, not our dog.

I used food to escape my pain, making lavish dinners, fancy snacks, and ordering in at least two times a week. "To help the local economy," I told myself.

In addition, the at-home workouts that kept me moving during lockdown were stressing me out because I didn't see any "results" from the work I was putting in. In fact, I gained about 20 pounds from March 2020 to January 2021.

It's a vicious cycle: work hard in a stressful job, splurge on food (or booze, or any vice) to forget that you're unhappy, and work out to assuage the guilt from splurging. All while barely meeting the rest of your basic needs.

I realized I'd been trapped in this same pattern of behavior since graduating with my MBA in 2016.

In March 2021, I was ready to break the cycle. I invested in a mindset coach, and the first draft of this book was written in a week-long personal development fervor. I was scared, excited, terrified, and beyond thankful that I finally had the means to do something to change my situation.

But in writing this book, I discovered that I had always looked for ways to change my situation.
I have been the $8 an hour barista and the $50,000 per year marketing manager.

I have worked four-hour days and 18-hour days.
I have had to work enough hours to qualify for medical benefits and not work enough to qualify for unemployment benefits.

In each position I've held, I've wanted to make my reality a little better because I knew, with un-wavering certainty, that it could be.

This book was designed with the essential worker in mind: the barista, the wait staff, the dishwash-er at the local bakery, the warehouse worker, the rideshare driver. The nurses, teachers, and jan-itorial staff rapidly adapted to changing times without missing a beat. Ten dollars equals about one hour of hard work and can be the difference between a trip to the grocery store and being late on your rent. This book is for everyone who thinks that change is too big a topic, too much work, or too expensive.

No matter who you are, where you work, or your particular situation, everyone can change their world.

Stephanie Cansian, May 2021

As of the publication of this book, I am living my dream of being a writer, and sharing my marketing and sales knowledge through my company, Say It Simply Productions.

All the weight I gained during that time I lost... and then some!
I know how scary it is to invest in yourself, how difficult it is to leave what you know. I am not recommending that anyone leave their job without a plan in place.

Instead, this book is asking you to take small steps outside of what's normal for you. Try something different to show yourself that you can improve your life, not by escaping it, but by enhancing it.

Then tell me all about how you changed your world. #Change1n10

Stephanie Cansian, November 2021

Tip #1

Try this first: Wake up really early, way earlier than anyone else you know. Do five push-ups, five sit-ups, and five burpees. Shower, and then write for 10 minutes about everything and anything on your mind at that moment. Do this sequence every day for a week. Do you notice a difference?

Tip #2

Take a free yoga class online
or see if your local community
center or library offers them as
part of their programming.

Tip #3

Identify a task you hate. Find someone who does that task really well, and ask them if they would teach you how to do that task better. Or just hire them.

Tip #4

Take a free meditation class.
There are plenty online or check
your local library.

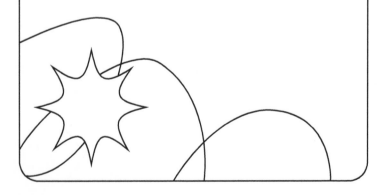

Tip #5

On a piece of scrap paper, write down the first name of a person who has wronged you. Rip it up. Write it again on another piece of scrap paper. Burn the paper (safely). Write the name down on another piece of scrap paper. Drown the paper in a bowl of water, and then bury it outside. Keep doing this sequence until you are tired and let the anger go.

Tip #6

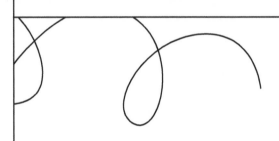

Learn origami. It's a more active meditation and dexterity practice. Plus, it's a neat way to send little notes!

Tip #7

Hide a $5 bill in your favorite book. Surprise yourself every time you read it.

Tip #8

Get rid of clutter you no longer
need by selling it on eBay.
You can also hire someone
to do this for you.

Tip #9

Find or buy a charming
keepsake box or two. Curate
the contents of the boxes with
your keepsakes and memories.
Make them your own personal
mini-museum detailing your
remarkable life so far.
Make sure to save room for
upcoming adventures!

Tip #10

Take a writing workshop.
Check your local library, school,
community center, or go online.

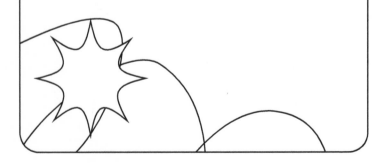

Tip #11

Write love notes to random items that capture your fancy, for example, a piece of art you are fascinated with, a meal your aunt cooked, or even a weird-looking set of bookends at a store. You can collect them in a notebook to look over when the world feels too gray. For example, I know that there is a plush toy espresso cup with a happy face somewhere in this world. Simply knowing it exists puts a smile on my face.

Tip #12

Cobble together a fruit basket made of whatever you have lying around. Then, pretend you are a Renaissance art student; sketch, draw, color, or paint a still life masterpiece for your mentor. Dressing the part is optional (but fun!)

Tip #13

Take a craft class at your local
library or community center.
You can also find tutorials for
specific crafts online.

Tip #14

DIY Shelving. I have made shelving out of milk crates, cardboard boxes, and dismantled desks. The physical act of putting things in their place instead of thrown around haphazardly makes the difference. Sometimes just displaying the items in your life in an organized way is enough to make you feel a little more focused, making the world feel a little brighter.

Tip #15

Go to a store that is redecorating and offer to take some of their display elements off their hands. When I was living with roommates, there was a store selling a solid wood armoire. They used it as a display, so it was scratched up and missing shelving but still worked! I bought it, and we used it as a super sophisticated coat closet in our duplex until the day it finally broke.

Tip #16

Get a bottle of clothing dye in your favorite color and a white tee shirt. Make yourself your favorite color shirt!

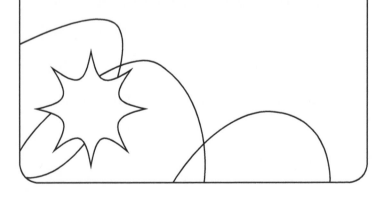

Tip #17

Treat your feet well! Make a foot scrub, or just soak them with some lovely soap at the end of the day. Make sure you have one really nice pair of socks or slippers to wear around the house. Don't forget a padded footrest for working at your desk! Splurge on pedicures, make an anklet, or get some toe rings to make your feet sparkle. Whatever makes you and your feet happy!

Tip #18

Try out a sleep monitoring device or app to see how well-rested you really are. The results might be eye-opening!

Tip #19

Buy a basic tarot deck and start
questioning the universe.

Tip #20

Buy one item for every sense: a sight that inspires you, a sound that energizes you, a smell that lifts your mood, something that feels invigorating in your hands, and food or drink that is guaranteed to get you moving with a smile, and not cause regret later on. These constant little reminders that life is beautiful are never bad things.

Tip #21

Buy a disposable fountain pen in a color you love. Carry it with you, and use it when you need to sign something. So fancy!

Tip #22

Go to a thrift store, goodwill, or consignment and buy a new outfit for yourself for $10.

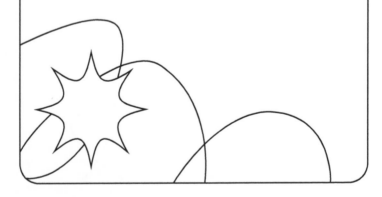

Tip #23

Get a pack of Magic Erasers
and make your sink and tub
or shower really shiny.

Tip #24

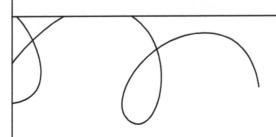

What can you glitter today?

Tip #25

Stickers, in general, tend to make life better. Buy some gorgeous stickers and put them on something boring that you see every day.

Tip #26

Buy a pocket-size yearly calendar and put a sticker or positive quote every day. This is an excellent exercise in developing a daily positive mindset.

Tip #27

Is there a cause or movement you believe in? Is there an organization that is fighting the good fight? If you can't donate, create a digital or physical poster that brings awareness to the cause. Share it with the organization and ask if they can use it. Donating time and creativity is just as important to a cause as money.

Tip #28

Buy some Grow Your Own kits and start a window garden of your favorite herbs!

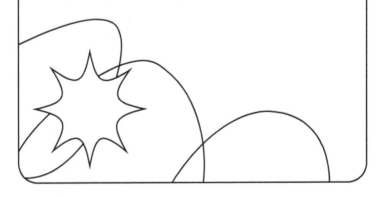

Tip #29

Trade wealth for a guardian to protect your sacred space. When I was 15, I found a funny lawn gnome at the local dollar store. Something about him just made me laugh, so I brought him home. He sat on my desk for decades and made sure I was working peacefully.

Tip #30

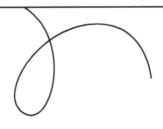

Buy a muse, an object that makes you smile and inspires you to create. The minute it no longer sparks, give it away as a gift to relight someone else's "muse fuse."

Tip #31

Buy one good pan and learn to cook your favorite foods in it.

Tip #32

If you struggle with picking and keeping fresh produce, take the thought out of it and get your greens and fruits shipped to you. They'll generally last longer because they have to ship, and you'll want to finish them before the next shipment arrives.

Tip #33

If you have the room in your budget, buy yourself a kit! Exercise your mind by learning a craft, completing a project, or solving a puzzle.

Tip #34

Make a list of places you could visit for $10 (gas, rideshare, bus, train, or subway). Now imagine you are a tourist seeing these places for the first time. Look for beautiful things you usually take for granted. Take pictures of them, sketch them, or jot down a note about them for later.

Tip #35

Test drive your dream car or bike.

Tip #36

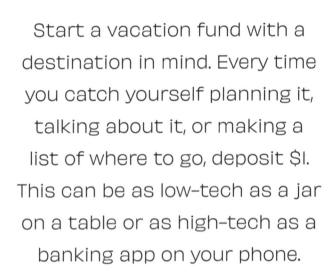

Start a vacation fund with a destination in mind. Every time you catch yourself planning it, talking about it, or making a list of where to go, deposit $1. This can be as low-tech as a jar on a table or as high-tech as a banking app on your phone.

Tip #37

Spend one week researching a cuisine you have never tried before. Bookmark recipes and look up ingredients if you are not familiar with them. Then try making one of the recipes. Eating cultural food is just as crucial as visiting, and gives you a "taste" of what you can expect when you go there!

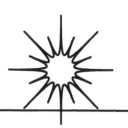

GIFTING

and

EXPERIENCES

Tip #38

Leave little love notes for your favorite people to find.

Tip #39

Leave a voice or video
message for someone
who could use a
pick-me-up.

Tip #40

Small gifts of kindness
can change the world, like giving
someone a pencil, paperclip,
or tissue when they really
need one.

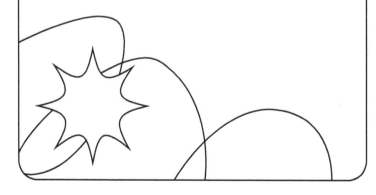

Tip #41

Buy a puzzle to do with friends.
Hide three of the pieces,
but leave clues in the box.
Surprise scavenger hunt!

Tip #42

Throw a poetry party! Everyone brings a snack and their favorite poem, memorized if possible. Then everyone goes around and reads or performs it and talks about why they love it afterward.

Tip #43

Buy or pick someone
a flower just because.

Tip #44

If you need to trim a collection, curate gifts to give to others. Example: lots of pens and notebooks? Make some fancy gift sets with a ribbon or twine for students or writers in your life! Lots of little makeup bags? Make your own soaps, balms, or scrubs, and make mini-spa gifts!

Tip #45

Get in touch with your favorite person's favorite podcast and ask if you can donate $10 for a quick shout-out to them. It never hurts to ask the question.

Tip #46

Host your own cooking
competition with your
foodie besties.

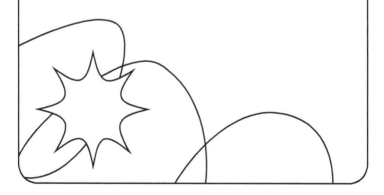

Tip #47

Buy a long-distance friend
one month's worth of a
streaming service and have
a weekly binge-watching
party with them.

Tip #48

Host a High Tea with finger sandwiches and desserts. Remember to dress fancy!

Tip #49

Make a list of five random things and see if you can find them while exploring a used bookstore or library.

Tip #50

Buy someone a book
(paper, eBook, or audio)
that will make them laugh loudly
and unexpectedly.

Tip #51

Buy some silk remnants, whole flaxseed, dried lavender, and a basic sewing kit. Make silk eye pillows for the headache and migraine sufferers in your life (don't forget one for yourself!)

Tip #52

Grow some mint (See Tip #28),
pick some, dry it, and put the
dried mint into tiny mason jars.
Instant Mint Tea gift
for the winter!

Tip #53

Go to a bank and trade one $10 bill for five $2 bills. Use them and note people's reactions.

Tip #54

Buy a loved one a book
(paper, audio, or eBook)
you think will change their life.

Tip #55

Buy a unique object at a thrift
store, create its backstory,
and post the story on the
website of your choosing.
Then try selling the item on eBay
or Etsy. Keep the money
or donate to a charity.

Tip #56

Buy $10 worth of different colored pens, anything but blue, black, and red. Whenever a coworker or friend asks to borrow one, assign them a color based on their personality.

Tip #57

Go to a store that's having a 10/$10 sale. Buy ten things, keep what you need, and give the rest as gifts or donations.

Tip #58

Buy a box of ramen
and make your own
10 Best Ramen Recipes.
Share your cookbook
with others!

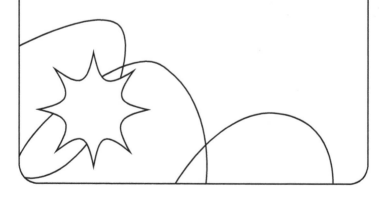

Tip #59

Pick up an impulse fashion accessory and have a five-minute fashion show.

Tip #60

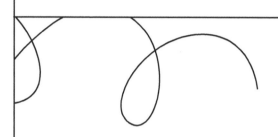

Buy a box of really fancy donuts.
Take some beautiful pictures
of them, then share them with
your besties.

Tip #61

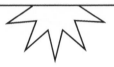

If you don't want the sugar,
buy an extra order of fries
to share. Some of the best
conversations start over a
shared order of fries.

CARING

for

OTHERS

Tip #62

Do you have a favorite barista or a favorite coffee shop? Try to tip your change on brewed coffee and bills for handmade drinks. If you can't afford to tip that day, make sure your favorite barista knows how much you enjoy your beverage and their skill in crafting it. Everyone loves specific positive feedback.

Tip #63

You can also buy the person
behind you a coffee.
It could make a difference
in someone's day!

Tip #64

Do you know an artist who is just starting out? Commission them to create an icon for you to use on social media. Make sure to credit and link back to the artist who made it!

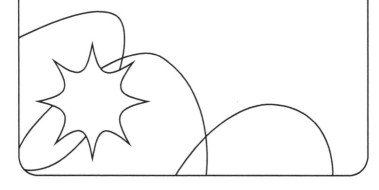

Tip #65

Is there a local business that you love and want to support? Ask them if they sell gift cards. Buy a $10 gift card once a month, and give them as gifts to people you think would love them as much as you!

Tip #66

Have extra fresh fruit or veggies on hand that you aren't going to eat? Donate it to a local soup kitchen or food bank.

Tip #67

Many teachers look for extra income during the summer months, and some will have unique skills and specialties. A former roommate of mine built and restored furniture during the summer. I offered to help him out if he would teach me how. I wound up learning how to refinish an old end table, and he got some help and company! Do you know anyone who could teach you a unique skill when they aren't working their main job?

Tip #68

There are many ways to support creators, artists, musicians, and writers online for as little as $1 per month. If you think that's not a lot, consider this: if 100 people gave an artist one dollar a month for one year, that's an extra $1,200. So never think that your donation is too small. There is no such thing.

Tip #69

Shop local when you can to support your local economy.

Tip #70

Is there a child in your life that you struggle to connect with? Try going to the local library with them and reading together. Your librarian can make suggestions for reading or introduce you to some programming that you can do together.

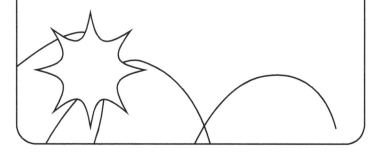

Tip #71

While you are at the library, why not pay off a stranger's fines? Then borrow a book or two to take home.

Tip #72

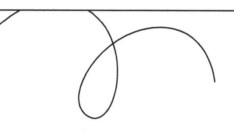

If reading is difficult, drawing and coloring together is also a fantastic activity. Afterward, you can take their drawings and turn them into stickers (see Tip #25).

Tip #73

You can donate to help
eliminate medical debt.

Tip #74

Did you just get your meal
for free? Why not tip what you
would have spent?

Tip #75

The next time you accidentally buy the wrong kind of socks, consider donating them to a shelter. Shelters are always in need of new socks, underwear, and feminine products.

Tip #76

Buy some funny or educational postcards and stamps. Mail them out to people in your life just to let them know you are thinking of them.

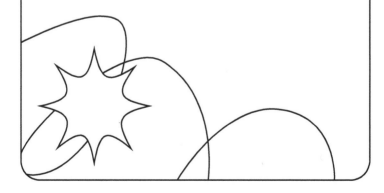

Tip #77

Hire a writer to create an elevator pitch on why the person you like should date you.

CARE

for   *the*

PLANET

Tip #78

Challenge yourself
to have more recycling
than garbage at the
end of the week.

Tip #79

Next level: composting. If you have a victory garden, there are both countertop and outdoor composters you can get. Or, if there is a local community garden or co-op, see if you can help volunteer and donate composted material.

Tip #80

Buying second-hand clothes is a powerful planet-saving move, but so is donating your old clothes. If you went thrifting (Tip #22), make sure you donate some clothing or shoes you no longer need. You can call your local shelters for drop-off times or ask family and friends if they want any items you have.

Tip #81

Volunteer to clean up a park or beach. An afternoon outside getting exercise and listening to an audiobook or podcasts can be its own reward.

Tip #82

Bring a friend to a park or beach clean-up, and make it a game! See who can collect the most or find the weirdest thing. Afterward, share a hot beverage and talk about what you found.

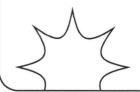

Tip #83

Buy bookmarks made of seed paper, and when you are done reading your book, plant the bookmark where you finished.

CARING *for* ANIMALS

Tip #84

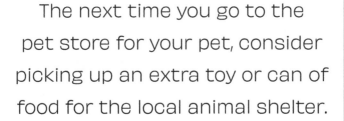

The next time you go to the pet store for your pet, consider picking up an extra toy or can of food for the local animal shelter.

Tip #85

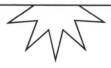

Want to take it one step further? Volunteer at a local shelter and help all those animals find their forever homes.

Tip #86

Is there a cat or dog problem where you live? Contact the local animal control and ask how you can help with their catch and release program.

Tip #87

Adopt a landmine sniffing rat.
These rats are trained to sniff
out landmines buried from past
wars so that farmers don't
get hurt. They save lives
and love snuggles.

Tip #88

The pangolin is one of the world's most trafficked animals and is considered critically endangered. You can symbolically adopt a pangolin through various rescue organizations.

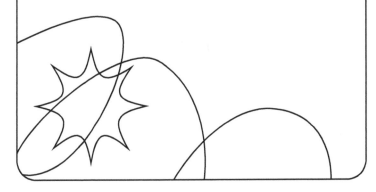

DEEP

DIVES

Tip #89

Buy a lovely smelling candle and build a playlist around it. Then have a self-date night with your favorite beverage and book.

Tip #90

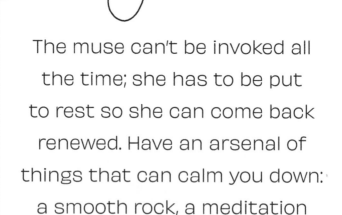

The muse can't be invoked all the time; she has to be put to rest so she can come back renewed. Have an arsenal of things that can calm you down: a smooth rock, a meditation pillow, or a tiny water garden.

Tip #91

If you have the extra money, treat yourself to a delivery service for your weekly food shop. This leads to fewer cars on the road, more time for you, and extra tip money into the local and gig economy.

Tip #92

Buy a makeup color that
you always wanted to try,
and buy the really good makeup
remover to go with it.

Tip #93

Buy yourself a bouquet.

Tip #94

The only bad foods are ones that will make you sick or will leave you with a deep feeling of regret. Avoid those, and everything else is fine in moderation.

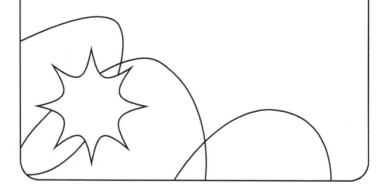

Tip #95

Make sure that if you treat yourself to some food, it's exceptional. You are worth it.

Tip #96

My first Friendsgiving was in a tiny apartment in a college town. My two roommates and I cooked, and we had my siblings and some friends over. I can't quite remember the menu, but I remember it being one of the best holidays I ever had. Good company can make a mediocre meal exceptional.

Tip #97

Here is a brutal truth: you are the product of the five people you talk with the most. Sometimes you will need to let people go in order to grow. And sometimes, people will need to let go of you. Both are uniquely painful experiences, but I promise they are survivable.

Tip #98

If you do not know your ultimate goal or your purpose, it's okay. Start with being the best version of you, and work on that every day.

Tip #99

Living day-to-day as your best self is good, but always have something to look forward to, even if you have to make up an occasion.

Tip #100

Buy this book for a friend and do it together! What can you learn and do a second time around?

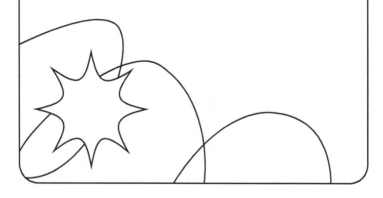

Thanks

One of the most important things you can have as a writer is a fantastic team of people complimenting you.

Thank you to my mindset coach Wes, writing coach Liz, and beta readers Kathleen and Ellen. Thank you to Lindsey, Andrew, and Lucy for taking my tiny book idea and making it a work of art!

Thank you Mom and Dad for always supporting me.

Thank you Matthew and Lauren for being great writers in your own right, and to Emily and Mikal for being the forces of nature keeping them in line.

And thank you to Kevin, my accountabilibuddy for life. I love you.

About the Author

Stephanie is a contributing writer on *Medium*, a marketing consultant, and a business coach who loves coffee, cooking, and pole dancing. She writes about work/life balance, personal development, and productivity while creating visual content for her business and personal enjoyment.

Stephanie can categorically confirm that Central Jersey exists, as she lives there with her husband and dog.

For more information, please visit
www.stephaniecansian.com

CPSIA information can be obtained
at www.ICGtesting.com
Printed in the USA
LVHW050444030322
712339LV00003B/218

9 798985 396911